H. G.

ALLEGRO RISOLUTO

Prepare:–
 Solo: Tuba
 Swell: 8ft. 4ft.
 Great: 8ft. 4ft. *f* + Sw.
 Choir: *mp* 8ft. 4ft. 2ft.
 Pedal: 16ft. 8ft. *f* + Gt.

See p. 32 for Editorial Note

Oxford University Press gratefully acknowledges financial support from the Percy Whitlock Trust
(http://www.percywhitlock.org.uk/) in printing this volume.

Reduce Gt. & Ped.

3

4

add to Gt.   add to Sw.

5

fix swell   Tuba   Gt.

reduce sw.

add to Gt.

6

add Full Sw.

Sw.

Gt.

Sw.

Dom W.

LANTANA

Prepare:—
Swell: Diap 8ft.
Great: Diap 8ft or soft reed
Choir: Flutes 8ft. 4ft.
Pedal: Sw. to Pedal only

J. H. R. D.

CHANTY

Prepare:–
Man. II 8ft. 4ft. 2ft. Flutes *mp*
Man. I   8ft. 4ft. Flutes *mf*
Pedal   16ft. 8ft. Flutes *mf* + Man. I

15

SALIX

Prepare:–
Solo: Cor Anglais 8ft. Flute 4ft.
Swell: Str. 8ft. Flutes 8ft. 4ft.
Great: Geigen+ Swell
Choir: Salicional 8ft. Flute 4ft.
Pedal: Soft 16ft.8ft.+ Choir

17

TOCCATA

Prepare:–
Solo : reed *mf*
Swell : 8ft. 4ft. 2ft.
Great: 8ft. 4ft. *f* + Sw.
Choir: 8ft. 4ft. 2ft. with soft 16ft.
Pedal: *mf* 16ft. 8ft. with Violone & soft reed

Choir legato

legato sempre

20

add to Pedal

legato

Choir

24

25

26

fix Swell

Gt.

Prepare Pedal *ff*

Gt. to Ped.

27

28

OXFORD UNIVERSITY PRESS

EDITORIAL NOTE

Chronologically, the *Plymouth Suite* was composed between the *Wessex Suite* for orchestra (July 1937) and the *Serenade for Strings* (February/April 1938). The first reference to the new suite appears in a letter from Whitlock to Leslie Barnard of 29 July 1937, and work on it was disrupted briefly from 30 August to 3 September by the I.A.O. Congress in Plymouth, which the Whitlocks attended.

Whitlock's diary notes that *Chanty* was completed on 20 September. The rest of the suite was finally completed on 1 December and the proofs were ready by the following April. There then followed a long gap of just over a year before it was finally published in May 1939.

However, Whitlock had already performed part of the work in public. A Bournemouth Pavilion organ recital programme for Sunday 14 November 1937 included 'Three Pieces from New Suite (*Allegretto; Lied; Shanty*)'. We can reasonably presume that *Allegretto* became *Salix*, *Lied* became *Lantana*, and *Shanty* was amended to *Chanty*.

The *Plymouth Suite* was put out of print in December 1970, although *Salix* and *Toccata* remained available as separate offprints. In addition, *Toccata* was included in *A Percy Whitlock Organ Album* (OUP, 1989).

Allegro Risoluto is dedicated to Harvey Grace (1874–1944), the President of the 1937 Incorporated Association of Organists' Congress at Plymouth. He and Whitlock first met in about 1917 when Whitlock took Grace on a tour of Rochester Castle. They next met in April 1936 in Chichester (where Grace was the cathedral organist). On this occasion Whitlock described Grace as 'v[ery] garrulous and rather exalted'. This opening movement is certainly very vigorous and uplifting.

Lantana is dedicated to Dom Winfrid, a monk and organist of Buckfast Abbey (né Joseph Rechtsteiner, 1879–1965). Whitlock first met him at Buckfast during an excursion from Plymouth. He described him thus: 'A raving [organ] enthusiast—he visits Compton's and bags parts to add to his organ!' He also explained that '*Lantana* signifies a "Wayfaring Tree", which is the nearest [title] I could get to its ambling style'.

Chanty is dedicated to James Hugh Reginald Dixon (1888–1976), organist of Lancaster Cathedral. This nautical movement was composed in response to Dr Dixon's own *An Organ Shanty*. Whitlock described him as 'generally the naughty boy at any party'.

Salix ('The Weeping Willow') is dedicated to Henry Austin Dewdney (1898–196?), a Bournemouth pianist, organist, and critic, who had 'something to do with most of the musical ventures in Bournemouth. A perpetual grouser, yet with much humour . . . . I should think he has the most influence of any of the local musicians.' Appropriately, this lovely movement has a rhythmic suggestion of *Sing all a green willow my garland must be* and melodic echoes of Percy Grainger's *My Robin is to the greenwood gone*.

Toccata is dedicated to Dr Harold George Moreton (1864–1961), borough organist of Plymouth, 'a sprightly old fellow [who] has been shabbily treated by the corporation, who are mercenary.' This *moto perpetuo* finishes off the set in fine style, with brilliant and striking effect when taken at the right speed.

This reprint contains a few amendments to the original edition of 1939. Although the original proof-reading (by Bernard Walker) was very good, some minor omissions have required attention. The most notable of these is in the final bar of *Chanty*, where the last two notes should also be played by the pedals.

MALCOLM RILEY
October 1989